PRICE 30 CENTS.

WEHMAN'S
BUDGET OF
JOKES

PUBLISHED BY
WEHMAN BROS.,
NEW YORK.

WEHMAN'S

BUDGET OF JOKES

REPLETE WITH

ENGLISH, IRISH AND GERMAN

WIT AND HUMOR

PUBLISHED BY
WEHMAN BROS.,
NEW YORK.

AUNT SALLY'S POLICY-PLAYERS' DREAM-BOOK.

PRICE 30 CENTS.

With this book you have a sure guide to lucky dreams and lucky numbers.

It gives you the true interpretation of dreams, and also the numbers in the lottery to which they apply; good combinations to play; significations of cards dreamed of, and their numbers; combination table for saddles, gigs and horses; table for finding lucky numbers; numbers of dreams of the months; for the days of the week; the Oraculam, or Napoleon Bonaparte's Book of Fate; the method of working the questions; the Oraculum table—in fact, this book gives all the sure signs. You can find out by any of these sure systems from this book whether you will be rich or poor; lucky or unlucky; whether you will get expected money, lovers, clothes, or any other article that you may set your mind upon. Do you dream of love or gold, or of friendship, of foes, or of life or of death? This book will explain everything clearly to you. You can tell your own fortune from its pages without consulting any living fortune-teller. Price **30 Cents** per copy, by mail, postpaid.

WEHMAN BROS.'
New Gipsy Dream-Book and Fortune-Teller

PRICE 15 CENTS.

This book gives the true interpretation of dreams, and the lucky numbers of the lottery to which they apply. It tells how to divine future events. How to tell fortunes by the grounds of coffee and tea-cups; by cards, dice, dominoes, etc. Physiognomy and physiology are treated; likewise charms, spells and incantations. It tells how to see a future husband; how to know whether a woman shall have the man she wishes; to know how soon a person will be married; to find out the two first letters of a wife's or husband's name; to know what fortune your future husband will have; to know your future husband's trade; for a girl to ascertain if she will soon marry; signs of a speedy marriage; signs to choose good husbands and wives; how to obtain happiness and affluence in the married state; predictions concerning children born on any day in the week, etc. Big value for little money. Price **15 Cents** per copy, by mail, postpaid. Address all orders to

WEHMAN BROS.,
158 PARK ROW, - NEW YORK CITY.

BUDGET OF JOKES.

"Why do they put the bracketed word 'laughter' after those jokes indulged in by so many public speakers?"

"Because they're funny. What should they put?"

"Why—WEHMAN'S BUDGET OF JOKES!"

This is as it should be, for on every page is that which will put you in the best of humor with yourself and the rest of mankind—and womankind, too

GOT THE WEIGHT.

Patrick was an employee in a grocery where the scarcity of help had compelled the grocer to take in an assistant who was entirely without experience. One day the grocer, in weighing out a purchase to a customer, searched in vain about the scales for something.

"Patrick!" he called out, "where is the pound weight?"

"The pound weight is it? Sure it's Misther Jones that has the pound weight."

"Mr. Jones has it? What do you mean?"

"An' sure, didn't ye till me to be perlite to the rigular customers?"

"Of course."

"Well, thin! Misther Jones comes in the day for a pound o' tay. An' says he, whin I axed him what quality o' tay he wud have. 'Whatever ye give me,' says he, 'give me the weight!' So I putt in the pound weight in the package wid the tay, perlite-like, an' it's himself that's gone wid it!"

THE COLOR LINE.

Trustee to colored party, who is starting for the water in bathing suit: "Can't you read the sign there?"

Colored Party: "Oi can, sor: 'Th' prisince av colored paple is not desired on this beach;' an' av yez'll lave me in th' water aboot tin minutes Oi'll kim out pfwhite as sand. Oi'm afther firin' th' 'licktrick light biler below."

Mistress—"Bridget, have you had a party of friends to supper? Or what is it that makes the kitchen in such a shocking mess?"

Bridget—"Please, ma'am, it was Miss Alice. She'd been learnin' at cooking school how to bile an egg, ma'am, an' she wanted to practice."

A SMALL CRIME.

O'Guff—"An' poor O'Giff got sixteen years in Sing Sing."

O'Gaff—"For phwhat?"

O'Guff—"For hommycide, I belave."

O'Gaff—"Oh, shure that's nothing; I thought it might be for killin' somebody."

HIGH SOCIETY SATIRE.

Gladys Groggan (patronizingly)—"I don't never see you to the theatre no more."

Genevieve Rafferty—"Bring a pair of oppry glasses and keep 'em squinting down at the parkay an' you'll see me."

ADVANTAGES OF EDUCATION.

"Why, Bridget," exclaimed the housewife, "I can write my name in the dust here."

"'Deed, ma'am," replied Bridget, admiringly, "thot's more nor I can do. There's nothin' loike education afther all, is there, ma'am?"

Conductor—"Look here, my man; what under heaven are you ringing the bell at both ends of the car for?"

O'Rafferty—"Sure, an' Oi want both inds of the car to stop."

IN THE THEATRE.

"Confound that woman and her hat!"

"Never mind, old man. Her halo in heaven will not be big enough to get in any one's way."

A BUSINESS MAN.

"Is Bronson as forgetful as ever?"

"More so. Why that fellow has to look himself up in the directory every night before he goes home from business. Forgets his address."

THE BEAUTY OF DYSPEPSIA.

"Mr. Trotter will take you in to dinner. He is a charming man, but a confirmed dyspeptic."

"Oh, how nice! He can do all the talking while I eat."

SHE PREFERS A DIFFERENT LIGHT.

"What kind o' fireworks are those?" asked Aunty Meddergrass of her city nephew, on the night of the Fourth.

"Those are Roman candles, Aunty."

"Are they? Well, I'm glad I don't live in Rome. I'd hate the worst kind to have to sew by the light of them things."

ONLY A SLIGHT ACQUAINTANCE.

De man dat's on handshakin' terms wid de debbil for six days ob de week, deah breddern, an' on Sunday jist fines time to bow to de Lawd, will discover, when he looks for recognishun on de las' day, dat de Lawd doan recollect him at all.

Jagson notes the tendency of the soaker to become a sponge.

It is always the man who doesn't shovel the dirt who is willing to give advice.

There are many men who are never ready to cut a caper of any kind till they get an edge on.

Because a young woman sees fit to wear suspenders is no reason for saying that she is a gallus girl.

The sphere of woman may indeed be boundless, but she has to stop when she comes to a barbed wire fence.

" This is an application for relief," as the man said when he stuck the porous plaster on his pain.

Mr. McFaddle—"Let me off at Miketown."
Conductor—"We don't stop; this is a through train."
Mr. McFaddle—"Thin, playse, sor, will yer sthop long enough fur me to tell Bridget that it's carried through I am."

Mrs. Mooney—"Yez don't hov Docther McCarthy any more?"
Mrs. Fagan—"No. Whin he was sick he called in anither docther. If he wouldn't trust himself to docther himself, Oi don't trust him to docther me."

Patrick has a great power of enjoyment after all, and always laughs at the right time. "One day he saw a bull attack a man, and had to hold on to his sides with both hands, the scene was so funny. After a little the animal turned his attention in another direction, and poor Patrick, after exploring the heights, came down with a thump on the other side of the fence. He rubbed his wounds, and as he trudged along the worse for wear, he said to himself, "Faith, I'm glad I had my laugh when I did, or I wouldn't have had it at all."

Mr. Muldoon—"Hullo, Pat, I hear yer workin'. How's that?"
Mr. O'Flaherty—"Yer roight. I'm workin' on half toime down to the coal yards. Half a loaf is better 'n none."
Mr. Muldoon—"Mabbe it is. But ye see, me boy, I'd rather loaf all the toime. Good day to ye, sor."

"That was a great down-fall," said the barber when he finished shaving the young man's upper lip.

There is not a man living who would not rather have finely chiseled features than have them cut by an awkward barber.

"Some boys thinks they is awful good 'cause their folks never misses church, rain or shine, but I notice, when they has a apple they never offers me a bite. They always chums with some boy wot's got poor front teeth."

"Where's Robinson?" "Left town." "Well, he's been bustling like the Old Scratch for a long time; 'spose he's gone to take a rest?" "No, he's gone to Canada to avoid arrest."

COMING ALONG SLOWLY.

"Were you ever in Philadelphia?"

"Yes. In 1846."

"You? Why you wern't born until 1862."

"I know it—but it was 1846 in Philadelphia when I was there."

MADE HER LOOK WELL.

Clara—"How well you looked on the street yesterday."

Maude—(immensely flattered)—"Do you really think so? I am awfully glad."

Clara—"Yes, you had on such a becoming Veil."

COULD'NT HEAR BOTH SIDES.

Miller—"I wonder why Jones was'nt appointed on the jury."

Muller—"He was rejected on the ground that he could'nt hear both sides."

Miller—"How so?"

Muller—"Why, he is deaf on one ear."

"Maud, run over to Mrs. DeSwelle's and tell her her chimney is on fire."

"I can't, papa. This is Wednesday, and Mrs. DeSwelle's day is Thursday. I'll go to-morrow."

The barber was addicted to habits of intemperance, so that on one occasion his hand was very unsteady at his work. In shaving the minister he inflicted a cut sufficiently deep to cover the lower part of the face with blood. The minister turned to the barber and said, in a tone of solemn severity:

"You see, Thomas, what comes of taking too much drink."

"Yes, sir," replied Thomas, "it do make the skin very tender."

Being out in a driving rain is not infrequently the forerunner of hoarse results.

"I hardly think I have any father, I hardly think I have any father," five year old Helen was heard repeating to herself.

"Why, my child, what are you saying?" asked her mother.

"Oh, I've got to learn it to please my Sunday School teacher. She says it's a prayer."

And so it was; but investigation proved it to begin: "I heartily thank thee, heavenly Father."

Husband—"What's that? Been shopping and bought $100 worth of silks? You said you were going for a drive."

Wife—"Yes, Cash & Co. advertised a great drive in dry goods."

Terwilliger—"Mrs. Playne does'nt like you, old fellow. She says you're a conceited popinjay."

Jerolomon—"The reason Miss Playne does'nt like me is because I am not a popin' jay."

A SURE REMOVER.

Mrs. Queasy—"I do wish I knew some way to remove freckles; my husband has them so bad it mortifies me to be seen on the street ith him."

Mrs. Shockem—"There is one thing will surely remove them."

Mrs. Queasy—"What is pray?"

Mrs. Shockem—"Arsenic, properly administered."

IT CAME TO HER EARS.

"I shall never ask a girl to marry me till I have seen the old man's check book."

So boasted I in company with some friends at a social gathering. Three years after I was reminded of it in a most awkward manner. I had fallen in love with and proposed to a young lady. When my proposal was over she rejected me, saying:

"You are very stupid, you know, for you have never seen the old man's check book, and are not likely to, for he is dead, and the check book is mine."

Theatre-goer—"The love scene in your play isn't half so natural as it used to be last season. The same people do it, too."

Manager—"Yes; but the lovers were married a few months ago."

Little Sadie—"O, Uncle Harry, Miss Brown and Mr. Swift are in the parlor, and she has her head on his shoulder."

Uncle Harry—"That's all right. She has a lien on him."

"George Washington must have been a mere boy when he was inaugurated President," said Mrs. Wilkins. "I saw an engraving of the scene the other day, and Washington was in short trousers."

When a holiday is most needed is the day after the holiday.

She—"I don't believe you love me as much as you did before we were married."

He—"Just as much as I ever did; perhaps not so much as I said I did."

Frenchman—"That lady to whom you introduced me is charming. Is she well connected?"

Chicagoan—"Well, I should say so. She's the wife of several of our first citizens."

Hicks—"There was a story afloat down town to-day that Jobson was embarrassed on account of the fall of May wheat."

Mrs. Hicks—"You don't say; who is she?"

"Why, Tommy Jones, shame on you! you didn't say all your prayers."

"Papa said I might leave out about our daily bread while mamma went to cooking school.

Mistress—"Well, Bridget, and how is your husband?"

Washerwoman—"Shure, an' he's all used up, mum."

Mistress—"Why, what ails him?"

Washerwoman—"Indade, thin, mum, last night he had sich bad dreams that he couldn't slape a wink all night, mum."

Quack—"So you prefer me to Dr. Bill?"

Mrs. Mulligan—"Och, indade, docther, dear, ye're a dale better than the other ould humbug."

Mike—"What soort of a dinner was it that ye had?"

Pete—"Well, it cost us tin dollars a plate."

Mike—"A coorse dinner, Pete?"

Pete—"Troth, it was that, bedad; 'twas the coorsest that iver I ate."

Mr. Manhattan Beach—"It is a very singular fact that no man who works in copper has ever had the cholera. I believe I'll get some preparation of copper from a drug store and take it every day if the cholera comes here."

Rafferty—"And phat the devil do ye make by that? Do you want to make a copper lightning rod of yourself and be struck dead by lightning every time there is a thunderbolt in the neighborhood?"

Clara—"Mr. Spudkins wants me to make a case for his umbrella, and I don't know what material to use."

Maude—"Why don't you use one of your silk stockings?"

Grace—"Miss Passé will catch cold if she sits on the piazza much longer."

Rosalie—"No, she won't. She's been trying for years to catch something."

Hymer—"Rather a thankless task, isn't it, writing poety for the papers?"

Rymer—"Thankless! No, indeed; thanks are about the only return I get."

Mrs. Newlove—"Charley, dear, I need one hundred dollars."

Mr. Newlove—"Do you, darling? How sympathetic you are! That's just what I need."

THE BITER BITTEN.

Glazebrook—"What do you think of that cigar?"

Grimshaw—"It's so good I'm sure you must have given me the wrong one."

SCANDAL WELL DEFINED.

Some pupils were asked by an examiner at a school examination whether they knew the meaning of the word "Scandal." One little girl held up her hand, and being told to answer the question she replied: "Nobody does nothing, and everybody goes telling of it everywhere."

DOMESTIC AMENITIES.

"Do you think, Charles, that that exceedingly short coat is a suitable garment to wear when out walking with me?"

"Yes, I'll concede it looked pretty short when I put it on, but you see I knew how very long it would be before you were ready to start."

All the men who wear yachting caps are not yachting captains.

No matter how little a man wants here below he never gets quite all of it.

Talking of the summer girl's bathing dress, if it costs so little how is it it comes so high?

"I don't care for lawn tennis," said the sky as it boosted the sun up a ways, "but I have a remarkably good blazer."

A postage stamp worth $1,500 has been discovered at Philadelphia. Any city that can lick that can now step up.

A number of students at Yale have been found guilty of cribbing at examinations. The Faculty should have put a Yale lock on the cribs.

"Can you suggest an inscription to go over the gate of the new cemetery," the president asked of the editor of the Quohosh *Bugle*.

"Let me see," replied the editor; "how will this do: 'We have come to stay?'"

"Why on earth do you have a melodeon instead of a piano, Mawson?"

"Because my daughter was so fond of music I couldn't get her to take any exercise. Now she gets the walk and music all at once."

"Do you see that remarkably tall young man over there, Miss Keenwit? Well, he was originally intended for the church."

"Indeed! I should have supposed him to have been intended for the steeple."

TURNS THEM DOWN.

A western editor is said to have hit upon a plan to keep subscriptions paid up that takes the cake. Every time a delinquent subscriber is mentioned in his paper, his name is inverted. For example:

ʃoɥu ʃouǝs and wife are spending a few days in Chicago.

Every other subscriber understands what it means, and there is a grand rush to get right side up again.

THE NEW YORK VERSION.

"The earth is the Lord's," but the down town sidewalks belong to the wholesale trade.

HOPS.

Pumps—"Do you like the hops at the Seaview House?"

Jumps—"No; I think they serve a very inferior quality of beer there."

A bishop was traveling along and encountered an old Irishman turning a windlass which hauled up ore out of a shaft. It was his work to do this all day long. His hat was off and the sun was pouring down on his unprotected head.

" Don't you know the sun will injure your brain if you expose it in that manner ?" said the good man.

The Irishman wiped the sweat off his forehead and looked-at the clergyman.   " Do ye think I'd be doin' this all day if I had any brains?" he said, and gave the handle another turn.

Officer Phelan—" Fwhat's all this row about ?"
Fiddsy, the Newsboy—"About over, of course !"

" A man may be drove to dhrink," said Officer McGobb, "but to git 'im away from it I find he has to be pulled."

" Father, how do you spell philosopher ? "
" Wid a large F of course, how else ? I wish yer wouldn't be botherin' me wid things yez ought to know yerself."

Pat—" Have yez an almanac, Moike ? "
Mike—" I have not."
Pat—" Thin we will have to take the weather as it comes."

" Are you pretty well acquainted with your mother tongue, my boy ?" asked the schoolmaster of the new scholar.
" Yes, sir," answered the lad timidly, "ma jaws me a good deal, sir."

Hicks—" We've got something new at our house—a machine to wash dishes."
Wicks—" And how does it work ?"
Hicks—" Beautifully. It breaks on an average five dishes a day. Fact; you would hardly know it from a hired girl."

" I don't feel right about going in there," said Chillson Feever in front of a physician's house.
"Pshaw ! He's one of the best doctors in the city," replied Coffin Coles.
" I know ; but look at his sign—'9 to 1'."
" Well ?"
" Well, I don't take any such chances as that."

The Skipper—" I say, guv'nor, you'd be more comfortable if you didn't lie on your stomach."
Feebly from the bottom of the boat—" Stomach—yes—fold it up, please, and—put it in the lining of my hat."

" Were you upset by the bank failure ? "
" Yes, I lost my balance."

There is a wide difference between horse sense and horse talk.

A cyclone is all that is necessary to raise a barn in the West.

An argument results from the collision of two trains of thought.

Modest bearing is very commendable in a man, but it is no recommendation to a fruit tree.

When a merchant gets down to business he is pretty sure of getting up in the world.

After a woman has passed a certain age she would just as soon get married on Friday as on any other day.

" The bride's father gave her away, did he not ? "
" More than that. He threw in $150,000 to boot."

" Are you busy ? " asked the Mug of the Growler.
" Busy is no name for it," replied the Growler ; " I'm rushed."

" I must have backed the wrong horse," said the amateur equestrian, as he landed on the top of his hat in the road.

Mamma—" How many sisters did your new playmate tell you he had."
Willis—" He's got one. He tried to catch me by saying he had two half-sisters, but he'll find out I've studied fractions."

Mrs. Meadow—"I hate to tell you, Mrs. Suburb, but, really, you ought to know it. Every time I've run in to the city lately I've met your husband on the return train ; and every time he was paying marked attention to some woman by his side, and every time it was a different woman. I've seen him with a dozen of 'em."
Mrs. Suburb (quietly)—" We have been trying to get a servant girl who would stay."

Farmer Roots—"I am sorry we let our daughter go to boarding school."
Mrs. Roots—" Why, Theobald ? "

Farmer Roots—"Wal, because it made her altogether too smart.
You know I gave her ten dollars last week and particularly cautioned
her to take care of it so's she'd have something to show for a rainy day.
What do you suppose she went and done?"

Mrs. Roots.—"I don't know."

Farmer Roots—"Bought four pairs of silk stockin's."

SCENE—INSIDE HORSECAR.

A two hundred pound old lady hanging by the strap and casting black
looks at an inoffensive but ungallant male beauty, who sits sucking the
head of his cane. A sudden lurch of the car flings the lady upon him
with great force.

"I say, dash it, don't you know," exclaimed the youth, "you've
crushed my foot to a jelly?"

"It's not the first time I've made calf's-foot jelly," was the answer.
And all the other people grinned, and were glad because it had not
happened to them.

GOOD FOR A DIFFERENT FARE.

Street Car Conductor—"That ticket is no good on this line, my
friend."

Passenger—"Why not?"

S. C. C.—The owners of this road are all married men and live at
home. That is a meal ticket."

A stranger, when dining at a foreign hotel, was accosted by a
detective who said to him:

"Beg your pardon, we are in search of an escaped convict, and, as a
matter of form, you will oblige me with your passport."

"Do I look like a convict?"

"Possibly not. In any case I shall require to see your passport."

The stranger, feeling annoyed, presented the officer with a bill of
fare, and the latter commenced to read: "Sheep's head, neck of mutton,
pig's feet."

"Very good," he observed; "the description tallies. You will
please come along with me."

She—"What superb teeth she has!"

He—"Yes, but they are false."

She—"Why do you think so?"

He—"She told my sister she inherited them from her mother."

A DEMONSTRATION.

Mrs. Frelter—"What do you think, my dear! Those two lovely
canaries of mine are dead."

Mr. Frelter—"You don't tell me! How do you account for it?"

Mrs. Frelter—"There's only one way to account for it. When your friend Profunds was here last night and sang that bass solo his jarring low C joggled the little darlings off their perch and I don't think they ever recovered from their fright."

Mr. Frelter—"Too bad! Then it's a real case of killing two birds with one's tone."

AN INHERITANCE.

Seeker—"I called on your friend Miss Gelid last evening. I must say that I never met a lady who was so adept in administering freezing glances."

Sageman—"That's the inheritance I was speaking to you of."

Seeker—"The inheritance?"

Sageman—"Yes. Her father was in the refrigerating business.'

A DISAGREEMENT.

Neighbor—"Why, how is this, Uncle Abner? When I saw you last week you were on trial for bigamy, with the evidence strongly against you. Is it possible that the jury disagreed?"

Abner—"Oh, no sah! De jury didn't disergree, but w'en dey said I wuz guilty I jus' disergreed merself an' lit out f'om dar whilst de sher'f wuz lickerin' wid de boys. I's like oner dese 'scape men' watches, sah. I knows how to go in good time."

WHY HE SAID GRACE.

Wagg—"I suppose Bulfinch is the most pious fellow I know."

Wooden—"Why, he never struck me that way. In fact I always thought him rather worldly."

Wagg—"Well, I happen to know for a fact that he never kisses his girl without saying grace."

Wooden—"Why, what in the world does he do that for?"

Wagg—"That's her name."

ALWAYS A WOMAN.

Mike O'Rafferty, pulling his wife out of the well—"Be gorra! a woman's at the bottom av iverything."

THE REIGN OF LABOR.

Mrs. Maloney—"And so yez wants to get a cook?"

Mrs. Wayup—"Yes, that is what I came here for."

Mrs. Maloney—"Well, have yez any riferinces."

SOMETHING LIKE AN IRISH BULL.

Two women were discussing a young man of their acquaintance whose father had been a distinguished member of the bar and a useful member of society. "For my part," said one, "I think George is very bright and capable. I am confident he will succeed." "Yes," replied the other, "he is undoubtedly a worthy young man; but I don't think he has head enough to fill his father's shoes."

"How polished Mr. Smithers is in his manner."

"Yes—its rather queer about Smithers. One so polished as he has no right to be so abominably dull."

Mrs. Campaigner—"Well, did the crowd enjoy your speech?"

Mr. Campaigner (home from a political rally)—"I guess they did. They ought to have enjoyed themselves. They all went down stairs to take a drink when I got up."

"Eb'nezah!"

"Ma'am?"

"Is yoh bin hookin watah millins f'um de mahkit?"

"No'm."

"Well, maybe yoh didn't. But I doan see how yoh am gwine ter prove an alibi fur dat colic."

AN EXCHANGE OF COMPLIMENTS.

Servant (delivering message)—"Mr. Triplett sends his compliments to Mr. Gazzam with the request that he shoot his dog, which is a nuisance in the neighborhood."

Gazzam—"Give Mr. Gazzam's compliments to Mr. Triplett, and ask him to kindly poison his daughter or burn up her piano."

HOW TO TELL BRIDE AND GROOM

He always carries two new grips and two umbrellas.

He always offers her his arm.

He's always clean shaven, and wears, besides immaculate linen, a careworn, worried expression.

He always pulls out his watch, presumably to see how much of the honeymoon is left.

When he registers at the hotel the "and wife" is written twice as large as his own name.

She never fails to ask how many lumps of sugar he takes in his coffee.

We may not love the barber, but we like to be next to him.

Jolliboy—"What do women do in their clubs? Do they tell bear stories and fishing lies, as men do?"

Miss Demure—"No; they tell mouse stories."

The most wonderful thing about a shad is how the meat ever got in between the bones.

Some of the people who are the most anxious about the recognition of friends in Heaven are the ones who shake hands with two fingers in church.

" The girl you were speaking to, Jack, seemed rather cold to you."
" Yes; she's an old flame."

TOO MUCH VARIETY.

" Ma," said a discouraged little urchin, " I ain't going to school any more."

" Why, dear ? " tenderly inquired his mother.

"'Cause 'taint any use. I can never learn to spell. The teacher keeps changing words on me all the time."

TOO MUCH ELOQUENCE.

Mr. Popinjay (falling on his knees)—" Miss Wilson, I can no longer resist the passionate impulse to appeal to you on the momentous subject that is fraught for me with the issues of life and death. And yet I am overawed at my presumption when I take into consideration the celestial glamour of your personal charms, the dazzling lustre of your intellectual attainments, the exquisite, the adorable——"

Miss Wilson—" Excuse me, Mr. Popinjay, but there are times when eloquence is rather out of place. If you wish to pop the question, pop it, and be done with it."

WHERE THEY DIFFERED.

Miss Goldburg—" I wouldn't marry you, sir, if you were as rich as Crœsus."

Mr. Hardrow—" Well, that's just the difference. I wouldn't marry you if you weren't."

" Milton's ' Paradise Lost ' is a noble poem, isn't it ? "
" Grand."
" Did you ever read it ? "
" No. Have you read it ? "
" No."

" How does your new errant boy go, Johnson ?"
" The long way, apparently, every time."

If you don't want your boy to turn out bad, don't bear down too hard on the grindstone.

There are people who think if they stand on the river bank and throw a straw to a drowning man they have done enough.

It is as bad to cover up the blind eye in a horse trade as it is to rob a man after you have knocked him down with a sandbag.

A FAIR PROPOSITION.

The tramp came up to the man on the corner and tackled him.

"Can you help one in need?" he said humbly.

"About how much this time?" was the inquiry following the appeal.

"Seven dollars."

The man on the corner jumped about seven feet high.

"Great snakes!" he exclaimed, "what are you going to do with all that money?"

"Get something to drink with it."

"It doesn't take that much, I hope."

"I don't know," and the tramp sighed wearily. "It's been so long since I've had a drink that I feel like I had a $7 thirst on me. Give me a chance to go and find out, and if I haven't I'll bring you back your change."

AT THE BASEBALL GAME.

Now doth the down town merchant gay
  Off from his office sneak,
On plea of illness dire at home,
  One afternoon each week;
And as he cheers the baseball game
  With loud, ecstatic joy,
He sees upon the bleaching boards
  His clerks and office boy!

HIS SUCCESSFUL BLUFF.

There is a maiden within the limits of greater Boston who blushes furiously at the mention of one little word of three letters—s—i—r. It is a short story. There was a little entertainment at the academy where Alice graduated. She attended, of course, and was introduced to a charming young man—an undergraduate. "He suggested that we stroll in the corridors," she said afterward to her most intimate friend, "and we talked about dances, the professors, and the same old things. Then he tried—oh, he must have forgotten himself, and I won't tell you what he tried to do. I wanted to bring him to his senses. 'Sir!' I said sternly, drawing myself up to my full height. Quicker than lightning he straightened himself and, with twice as much dignity as I had, said in a tone of freezing interrogation, 'Madam?' I almost fell through the floor. I had not been doing a thing and he knew it, but I blushed and felt as cheap as if I had tried to—to put my arm around his waist."

True to the nature of the beast, many a man who in his time has cast sheep's eyes at a pretty girl, has afterwards had the wool pulled over them.

There is no middle course for the average man during housecleaning time.   He must be either a poltroon or a hero.

"That's a very neat turnout," said the young woman's father as Augustus sped from the door.

Visitor—"I suppose you have to be constantly on the alert to prevent the escape of the lunatics."

Insane Asylum Attendant—"Yes; nearly all of them are just crazy to get out."

"So you married Smith's widow.   Did he leave anything?"
"Nothing but her, and I wish he hadn't."

A capital story is current in London about two Waterford merchants and hatters who once obtained an audience with the present Pope's predecessor.   They were old-fashioned men and good, pious Catholics, and when, after much formality, they were ushered into the room where Pius IX., in all his Papal splendor, was waiting to receive them, both were so overcome with emotion that they could do nothing but stare in blank amazement, trembling all over.   At last one of them found his tongue.   Throwing himself on his knees he shouted out loud enough to be heard in every corner of the vast chamber: "O Holy Father, we're from Waterford!"

"Have yez had a vacation this year?"
"Oi hev—tin weeks"
"Howly Moses! What fer a boss have yez?"
"A mighty bad man. I wor on sthrike."

"No; the shortest courtships are among the Irish.
"? ?"
"They no sooner meet than they 'mate.'"

A Dublin doctor sent in a bill to a lady which ran thus: "To curing your husband till he died."

"Have you got through cleaning, Bridget?"
"No, mum, not intoirely. I've scoured the bookcase and pianny, and I'm just going down suller for more sand to begin on the rist of the furniture."

Mother (wrathfully)—"Didn't Oi tell yez not to play wid dot McGeachy boy?"

Boy (woefully)—"I ain't; he's been playing wid me."

WHAT HE WANTED TO KNOW.

Travers—"I hear that you invited Miss Summit to the theatre the other night."

Dashaway—"Yes."

Travers—"And she didn't accept?"

Dashaway—"No."

Travers—"You haven't got the money about you, have you?"

WOMAN'S WAY.

Husband—"I am not ready to go out walking yet."

Wife—"But I am, and we must go immediately."

Husband—"But, my dear, your hat is not on straight."

Wife—"Dear me! Isn't it? Wait a minute till I go to my room and fix it." (Exit wife for half an hour, and her shrewd husband completes his work.)

UNNECESSARY EVIDENCE.

Smith—"You needn't tell me that dogs don't know as much as human beings. I took Ponto to church with me last Sunday."

Jones—"Yes?"

Smith—"Well, sir; he slept through the whole sermon."

"Do you like me?" asked the young man, addressing the little brother of the young lady on whom he was making a call.

"I don't like you as well as I like Jack Joliboy."

"Why not?"

"Because he always gives me ten cents to go out of the room when he comes to see sister."

"Why, you have no servants at all in your house now."

"No."

"What has become of your hired man?"

"My husband fired him—whiskey."

"And your hired girl."

"She fired herself—kerosene."

"You have got a new hired girl, I see, Mrs. Youngwife?"

"Yes; I got her about a week ago."

"How do you like her?"

"Very much indeed. She lets me do almost as I like about the house."

"I am at your service, ma'am," as the burglar said when the lady of the house caught him stealing her silver.

It was a very tender hearted lady who refused to strike an octave.

When it comes to talking of this country's crops, the hair cutting barber unquestionably stands at the head.

What troubles the housekeeper is the thought that the minute the furnace stops eating up coal the refrigerator will begin eating up ice.

A Boston paper prints an essay entitled "What Shall We Eat For Dinner?" That question has bothered millions of poor devils for ages.

When we hear that a man has a spice of deviltry in him we naturally rush to the conclusion that there is something cloven about him.

To make himself solid with the gang the politician must set up the liquids.

A fellow can't get a pull unless he has some push about him.

It isn't much trouble for a man to make his mark in politics—the trouble is in removing it.

When one jumps at a conclusion he rarely catches it.

If the corner of your building sags, something to stay it is the propper thing.

The trouble with the sober second thought is that it so often has the bust head as a result of the first thought's actions.

Sailboats are sometimes upset by a squall; and the same catastrophe occasionally visits young paterfamilias.

Friend—"Why don't you write a joke on the ice bill?"
Humorist (savagely)—"I guess not I've just paid one."

PERFECTLY SAFE.

Young Saphead—"Do you know, Miss Smilax, my friend Charlie Bighead has got brain fever. Do think I'll ever have it?"
Miss Smilax—"Well, not as you are now."

KNEW THE FAIR SEX.

Head Salesman — "That last lot of sunshades doesn't seem to go. "
Proprietor — "What's the price of them?"
Head Salesman — "Two dollars apiece."
Proprietor — "Mark them down to $1.99 and put an extra salesman on that counter to attend to the rush."

CUE RIOUS.

Podgers says that his baby can beat any expert billiard player — he can bawl without a cue.

Hairdresser — "Any bay rum, sir?"
Middy — "Thank you — a — no! Not quite so early in the morning you know!"

Daughter — "Mamma, shall I marry the millionaire I don't love or the poor man I do love?"
Mamma — "By all means, dear, marry the man you love."

"There's nothing like poached eggs," as the man said when he robbed his neighbor's hen house.

When the regular patron goes to the barber shop he can see his own mug without looking in the mirror.

"So you want to sing in the choir?"
"Yes."
"What part?"
"Well, I went in as first base, but they changed it to short stop when they heard my voice."

Men of the highest respectability sometimes stand in front of a soda fountain and deliberately wink at a violation of the law.

It isn't every man with a husky voice who can pass as a farmer.

Public singers who sign soap recommendations seek a baubled reputation.

There are people who seem to lose all their religion the minute they can't have their own way.

When a man says he is badly cut up it is fair to presume he has received hash treatment.

Mamie—" Two hundred and eight."

Teacher—" Wrong; You have only 207."

Mamie (triumphantly)—" Yes, but I swallowed a fishbone at breakfast this morning."

OFF COLOR.

Lipsley—" You know those cigars Miss Beacon sent me for Christmas ? "

. Lapsley—" Yes."

Lipsley—" Well, I gave a lot to my friends, and now I haven't any left."

Lapsley—" What, cigars ? "

Lipsley—" No, friends."

HE MEANT IT, TOO.

" Well, little boy, what's your name ? "

" Shadrach Nebuchadnezzer Jones."

" Who gave you that name ? "

" I don't know. But yer bet cher life if I find out, when I gets me growth they'll be sorry for it."

AMERICAN STYLE.

Scads—" You say he left no money ! "

Baggs—" No. You see he lost his health getting *wealthy*, and then lost his wealth trying to get *healthy*."

A little girl, whose attention was called to the fact that she had forgotten to say her grace before beginning her meal, shut her eyes meekly, and said, " Excuse me. Amen."

It is a well established principle of economics that the young man who would get up with the sun should not stay up later than ten o'clock with the daughter.

Clerk—" Here's a health item in this paper that I believe I'll work up into a placard to hang up in the hat department—next to " No Trouble to Show Goods."

Proprietors—" What is it ? "

Clerk—" Don't Go Out Without a Hat."

Employer—" Can't you get here earlier mornings ? "

Boy—" Yes, sir ; when the wind is at my back."

Mrs. Watts—" Mary Ann, these balusters seem always dusty. I was at Mrs. Johnsons to-day and her stair rails are clean and as smooth as glass."

Mary Ann—" Yis, mum. She has three small boys."

Mrs. Topflat "Bridget, where did you get that dreadful eye."

Bridget Me brother gave it to me, mum; and what'll the neighbors say? Me with an eye like that and no husband."

Prisoner "Would you believe this man on oath?"

Paddy O'Reilly "Not onless he wor lyin', yer Honor."

Boarder "Are these the French sardines that you have given me?"

Irish Waiter "Now, as to that I couldn't say, for they were pasht shpaking whin we opened the box."

ONLY ONE FAULT.

She can fix her hair in fashion, and her manner's rather dashing, and
her dainty little shoes are just in style;

She can jabber French and German, and expound upon a sermon, and
set a person crazy with her smile.

In the tastes that are æsthetic, and in mixing face cosmetic, they say
she has no equal anywhere.

And in chewing tutti frutti she enhances much her beauty, and the
settings in her teeth are very rare.

She can thump a grand piano, and can sing in great crescendo, and
her style of elocution's very trim;

She has college education, is the pride of her relation, but she still
persists in saying " It is him."

THE AGE TO REFORM.

A father had been lecturing his young hopeful upon the evils of
staying out late at night and getting up late in the morning.

"You will never amount to anything," he continued, "unless you
turn over a new leaf. Remember that the early bird catches the
worm."

"How about the worm, father?" inquired the young man.   "Wasn't
he rather foolish to get up so early?"

"My son," replied the father solemnly, "that worm hadn't been to
bed all night; he was on his way home."

A LITTLE BIT PROUD.

Customer—"I'd like to have you be extra particular in dressing that
fish "

Fishmonger—"Yes sir."

Customer—"Because I don't want to be seen on the streets with a
fish, unless it's as well dressed as I am."

THE LAST DIVISION.

Teacher—"If your mother should wish to give each one an equal
amount of meat, and there should be eight in the family, how many
pieces would she cut?"

Class—" Eight."

Teacher—"Correct. Now each piece would be one-eighth of the whole. Remember that."

Class—"Yes'm."

Teacher—" Suppose each piece were cut again. What would result?"

Smart Boy—" Sixteenths."

Teacher—"Correct. And if cut again?"

Boy—" Thirty-seconds."

Teacher—" Correct. Now, suppose we should cut each of the thirty-two pieces again, what would result?"

Little Girl—" Hash."

ENTITLED TO SYMPATHY.

Mendicant—" Would you please be so kind as to give me a four-button cutaway suit of clothes? I'm an old soldier. I had a good job, but I got discharged last year."

Man—" What were you discharged for?"

Mendicant—" Soldiering."

IT WOULDN'T DO.

" My motto is 'live and let live,'" said young Dr. Squills, just graduated.

" Unpractical, unpractical. You'd better adopt some other," said Dr. Pills, more experienced.

" Johnny," said his mother, "if you don't quit smoking cigarettes you won't grow a bit."

" Don't care if I don't," responded Johnny sullenly.

" And, of course," continued the good woman, " If you don't get any bigger you will still have to wear clothes made from your father's old ones."

" I guess I'll quit ma."

Hicks—" Do you know where they get isinglass?"

Mrs. Hicks—" No, nor care; I wouldn't wear one."

" That's a queer conceit of Dr. Johnson's, that 'words are men's daughters!'"

" Natural enough—they're so oft a-miss."

" How benevolent you are getting!" observed a visiting friend, as the other tossed a dime to an organ grinder.

" Yes," was the reply; " not a dago's past but I give something to the poor."

" There's one strange thing about our soprano."

" No; you don't say so! What is it?"

" Merely that her solo is always so high."

Mr. Tile—"Your wife used to lecture before she was married; has she given it up now?"

Mr. Milds—"Well—er—yes; that is, in public."

Friend—"Do you permit your wife to have her own way?"

Husband (positively)—"No, sir. She has it without my permission."

Mr. Brink—"What was the most expensive piece of jewelry you ever bought?"

Mr. de Vorce—"My wedding ring. I'm paying forty dollars a week alimony."

Mr. Pugh—"Never saw such a crowd at our church before."

Mrs. Pugh—"New minister?"

Mr. Pugh—"No; it was burned down last night."

Mr. Grumpps—"The *Ladies Journal* says a woman should make herself as attractive to her husband after marriage as she did before."

Mrs. Grumpps—"Huh! My father always gave me plenty of money to make myself attractive with. You don't."

Husband—"My dear, women have such small minds."

Wife—"Well, I don't know that it is to be wondered at, considering that they need to give their husbands a piece of it so often. The greatest wonder is that they have any minds at all."

To prove that the clothes he sells are wool, a dealer shows customers the moths in the garments.

Parent—"Young man, I have noticed that you are paying attention to my daughter. Now, is it all on the square?"

Lover—"No——it's mostly on the stoop."

He (poet)—"Didn't you know that poets were born?"

She—"No. I always considered them as the ones that bore."

Primus—"Nixon's salary is raised. His employer saw him refuse to go into a barroom with a friend."

Secundus—"It was a matter of principle with Nixon, I suppose?"

Primus—"Yes; it was his turn to treat."

The summer girl has to put up with many a rain beau.

"I am banking on you," as the farmer said as he proceeded to hill up his potatoes.

McFingle (at the seashore)—"Ah, see that Chinaman standing on the beach. Hello, John, what are the wild waves saying?"

Quong Fung—"Washee, washee!"

Jacques—"Mabel, I feel very brave to-day; I think now is a good time for me to see your father."

Mabel—"Well, I don't believe I would to-day."

Jacques—"Why not?"

Mabel—"You'd better wait till you have your old clothes on."

Riggs—"How long has your wife kept servants?"

Jiggs—"Two weeks some times."

"And so you left your place through having words with your mistress."

"Well, mum, not words, mum—not adzactly what you might call words mum. I only spoke to her as one lady might to another."

Merritt—"That was a pretty hard doctor's bill I had to pay."

DeGaray—"How was that?"

Merritt—"You see it was for injuries I received by being thrown from a horse I was riding by the doctor's advice."

"Mr. Henpekt loved the woman he married so much during court-ship that he had no peace of mind until he made her his wife."

"Has he peace of mind now?"

"No, he has a piece of hers every day."

"Jack Wilkins broke his bicycle yesterday."

"Lucky fellow," replied Willie Wishington, "Mine is as wild as it was the first day I twied to wide it."

HE WAS THE BIG PARTY HIMSELF.

A story is told of a gentleman prominently connected with one of the big foundries in Pittsburg. The gentleman in question is an unusually large man, very tall and far around. Finding himself caught in a little town about twenty-five miles from Pittsburg one night, with no train going to the city, and being very anxious to reach there at 11 o'clock, he wired to an express down the track to stop for him.

"We stop for officials only," came the answer.

Quick as a flash went the second telegram.

"Will you stop for a large party?"

"Yes," was the reply, and the long express slowed up and stopped when it reached the little town, and the gentleman complacently stepped aboard.

"Where is the large party?" inquired the conductor, with wide open, astonished eyes as he gazed about the empty depot.

" Ain't I large enough ? " chuckled the delighted new passenger.

The conductor glared, and then burst into a hearty laugh as the fitness of the application burst upon him.

ADAM'S ADVANTAGE.

Rowley—" There is one satisfaction that Adam had as a gardener."

Surface—" What was that ? "

Rowley—" He didn't have neighbors who raised hens."

Marian—" Which would you rather be—independently rich or happily married ? "

Lillian—" Independently rich, for then I should get happily married."

Miss Thin—" Don't you think my new dress is just exquisite ? They all say so."

Fanny—" O, lovely! I think that dressmaker of yours could make a clothes pole look quite graceful."

Bleecker—" Who is your favorite novelist ? "

Miss Backbay—" Howells."

Bleecker—" Great Scott ! "

Miss Backbay—" Some affect to think so; still I prefer Howells."

It often happens that a fellow who "won't go home till morning " can't go home then until somebody pays a fine for him.

ECONOMY IS WEALTH.

" He's an economical man."

" How does he show it ? "

" He wanted a sign prohibiting fishing on his place, so he took a board out of an old bale he had with ' Use no hooks ' painted on it, and put that up."

ACCOMMODATING.

" You hold my future happiness," he whispered.

" Well," she answered, pleasantly, " I'll let it go."

LIKED CHILDREN.

Neighbor No. 1—" Does the noise of my children disturb you ? "

Neighbor No. 2—" Oh, I like it."

" Do you really ? "

" Yes, indeed. My husband's relatives are rather nervous people, and they never stay longer than a day or two now."

Mudge—"Were you at the races yesterday?"
Yabsley—"No."
Mudge—"Then I guess you've got it."
Yabsley—"Got what?"
Mudge—"Five dollars. I need it."

Mrs. Grimley—"Our iceman is very strong. He carried 500 pounds of ice from the street to-day clear into our cellar. Isn't that wonderful?"
Mr. Grimley—"No, not if he weighed the ice himself."

They are called racing tips because their patrons are so easily upset by them.

The man who has "the pull" at a picnic is generally the thoughtful chap who has brought a flask.

Counting the chickens before they are hatched is the highest way of showing confidence in the reliability of the hen.

The minister didn't think how it sounded when he said the dead shoemaker had been faithful unto the last.

Bella—"You should have seen the crowds of men calling in the box I was in last night."
Stella (with great sweetness)—"Who occupied the box with you?"

A woman in Dexter, Me., who became a convert to the faith-cure belief six months ago, put away her false teeth, confident that new ones would sprout naturally. Since she cut her store teeth, however, she has felt no others gumming along.

Maud—"Do you suppose that all the creatures that go out between the acts go to see real sure-enough men?"
May—"No, indeed; most of the time its only spirits."

People who are all the time talking about charity beginning at home are not the ones to do very much to help her get a start.

He—"Don't you think I'm rather good looking?"
She—"In a way."
He—"What kind of a way?"
She—"Away off."

Visitor—"I can't understand why you have no telephone here?"
Club Man—"The majority of our members are married."

" Why does Miss S. address all her verses to the moon? "

" Well, I suppose it is because the man up there is the only one who can't run away."

" Then the guests went home and the neighbors went to sleep," is the way a local weekly winds up its account of a lively party given down-town.

Report comes from London of the discovery of the thistle as an article of food for man as well as beast.   The thistle has certainly some very fine points.

Speaking of small pieces of ice, it's generally a warm day when it's left.

A boy is never of any use until he has discovered that he is not a success as a whistler.

Tommy—" Pa, may I ask you a question? "
Pa—" Certainly, my child."
Tommy—" Well, where is the wind when it doesn't blow? "

When a French editor gets mad he always dips his pen in gaul.

Is the fellow who " paints the town red " guilty of a cardinal sin?

It was about time that corn should take a drop.   It has been the cause of people's taking a drop to much long enough.

The way to nail a lie is to pin the man down to facts.

Jagson says it is absurd for a man to try to get any lien on a fat office.

The first doctor of divinity is understood to have been O. Fiddle, D. D.

A blush on the cheek is not the same thing as a red nose, but it's the next thing to it.

A thoughtful Philadelphia capitalist keeps a cool thousand on his desk during hot days, thus saving the expense of an electric fan.

The papers are mentioning as an item of news that the typewriter girls are forming a union—just as though the typewriter girls hadn't been busily forming unions ever since they became an institution.

3

First Chicago Girl—"Mrs. Slumkins is a widow, is she not?"
Second Chicago Girl—"Only temporarily."

Some cheap perfumes are not to be sniffed at.

The minister's wife (to industrial scholar).—"Eliza Jane, I am sorry to hear from your schoolmistress you are not diligent at your needlework. 'You know who it is finds work for idle hands to do?'"
Eliza Jane (intensely anxious to propitiate)—"Yes'm; please'm, you do!"

Successful Lawyer—"Always remember, young man—'There's plenty of room at the top.'"
Student—"But I want to be a lawyer. I'm not studying for a hotel clerk."

"Mr. Tilbow called to-day and returned the umbrella you loaned him last week."
"Did, eh? Well by Jove! I wonder what game that fellow is trying to play on me."

HE WOULD.

Diggs—"I shall make a sensation among the dudes at the mask ball."
Figgs—"What will be your disguise?"
Diggs—"I am going as a tailor's bill collector."

HOLDING BACK.

Witherby—"There's a button almost off your coat, old man. You ought to call your wife's attention to it."
Von Blumer (sadly)—"I'm going to, as soon as I can save up enough money to get her a new gown."

THE TIME FIXED.

"Miss Twilling," said Mr. Calloway, glancing down at his polished boots with a self-satisfied air, "don't you like to see a man always looking as if he had stepped out of a bandbox, his clothes nicely brushed, and everything about him indicating refinement?"
"Yes, Mr. Calloway, I do," replied Miss Twilling, glancing at him significantly, "I like to see such a man as you have described about once a year."

WANTED HER OPINION.

She—"Your roommate called on me last night."
He—"How did you like my new dress suit."

Fred—"There seems to be a lot more fuss made of Miss A.'s singing than Miss K.'s, and I am sure Miss K. has by far the richer voice."

Jack—"Oh, yes, but Miss A. has by far the richer father."

He—"Going into the surf this morning, Miss Mary?"

She—"Yes, I think so. Are you?"

He—"No, I think not. Fact is, I'm afraid of the sea puss."

She—"Why, are there cat-fish about here?"

"Is the drum fish good eating, pop?"

"No, Willie, it's very easy to beat it."

It will be a proof that human and brute lives run parallel in some ways if that new cattle disease, "swelled head," is traceable to the "horns" in the case.

THE FATAL (GERMAN) NIGHT SHIRT.

[A LONG WAY AFTER HOOD'S SONG.]

Now listen, all ye gentlefolks, as I my story tell;
About ye gusset, band, and yoke, ye seam, and tuck, and fell,
And neck and collar, all in one, and eke ye armholes wide,
About a famous German shirt, its wearer, and his bride.

In Holland on a lovely day ('twas bright as bright could be),
A bride and groom of German birth, went up the Zuyder Zee,
They had been married that same day, as you could plainly see;
Her head upon his shoulder lay, his hand lay on her knee.

"Mein lieber Frau, I ish so glad to have you safely here:
Althou I takes you from your dad, you nothing has to fear,
See! here we ish at Amsterdam, ve takes no more dis boat;
But goes to the hotel (by tâm! more better as a float)."

Now Heinrich loved his lager-beer und Barbara liked her pretzel;
So Heinrich roar'd out, "Komm-ze hier, and wait upon my vestal;
Und take this little trunk up-stairs, and keep it in a room;
Mein Gott! I specks I never cares if ten o'clock comes soon."

Now, Barbara and her Heinrich dear, they had a jolly supper,
They supped of bliss and lager-beer, and read the poet Tupper,
And just at ten she went to bed, her face was like a rose,
And 'xactly like a small dew-drop was a tear upon her nose.

Und Heinrich counted forty-two, and scrambled up the stairs:
Und when he gets into the room, all off his clothes he tears;
Except a great long Hamburg shirt, Tannhäuser! it was long—
It touched his chin, it touched the ground, and dragged its length along.

Und Barbara peeped from 'neath the clothes, und thought it was a ghost;
Und was so scared, she never rose but died, just like a post.
Und Coroner said: "Heinrich, my boy, I hate to be uncivil,
But in that shirt, I'm blessed if you don't look just like the devil!"

So Heinrich mourned his wife one year; und then he got anoder:
But thinking of his shirt, he tried a great big sob to smother.
And to his Fräulein he did say: "No more I looks like ghost;
I got a Yankee shirt to-day, as good as nix, almost."

"But should you fear poor Barbara's fate, I tells you what you do—
You pulls the bedclothes o'er your head, and (whatever else you do)
Just wait until der light ish out, and then your eyes you ope—
You will not know if I'se a ghost, or Luther, or the Pope."

A SETTLER.

"Heh, you feller! Come back und settle for dot beer!"
The Tough Customer (making his exit)—"Ah, come off! Didn't
yer say de frot' 'd settle?"

The Sword Swallower—"I have had notice that they don't want me
any longer in the museum."
Fat Woman—"Well, who will take your place?"
Sword Swallower—"Why, a girl from Boston is going to swallow her
words."

The young man in love doesn't care so much about having a yacht at
sea as having a little smack ashore.

"Yes," said the old lady, "they've had a dry season out there—they
have had to irritate the land."

The auctioneer is the only man who likes to see his customers wear
a forbidding aspect.

The shoemaker is a man who frequently gets "beaten out of his
boots."

Harry—"Blowitz proved to his wife that he didn't marry her for her
money."
Jack—"How?"
Harry—"To show her how little he cared for it, he spent every cent
she had."

"Alas! the lost caws," murmured the crow as his companion fell, a
victim to the shotgun policy.

Lady (with high hat)—" I beg your pardon, but I forgot my opera glass. Would you kindly lend me yours just a moment?"

Tyrant man (in seat behind)—"Very sorry, madam, but I need it to sit on."

"What has become of the big man who used to beat the bass drum?" asked the private of the drum-major.

"He quit us about three months ago."

"Good drummer, too, wasn't he?"

"Yes, very good; but he got so fat that when he marched he couldn't hit the drum in the middle."

TWO GOOD RULES.

Reggy Westend—" Col. Deeply says it's his rule 'Never to take a drink when you feel as if you need one;' and old Baxter says 'Never take a drink except when you need one.' Now what is a fellow going to do?"

Jack Lever—"Follow both rules, Reggy, and you'll be all right."

THAT WOULD BE BAD.

Gummey—"It would never do to have girls on the police force."

Gargoyle—"Why wouldn't it?"

Gummey—"You see, every arrest they would make would be a miss-apprehension."

HAD TAKEN IT.

Railway King—"What do you think I need, doctor, to set me up again?"

Doctor—"Well, I think a little iron will help you."

Railway King—"Good. I gobbled up a whole railroad system last week."

"Will you love me when I'm old," simpered gay Miss Oldgirl to her youthful intended.

"Why, my darling, I do," responded he in mild surprise.

"The style of writing that you do must be very hard work."

"Well, it is; but what made you think of it?"

"Why, it makes me tired to read it."

The tramp may be all wool and a yard wide, but he is goods that will not wash.

"I got an awful fright last night," said Jennie.

"You did?"

"Yes; when George was going away he took my hand to bid me good night."

"And you thought he was going to kiss you?"

"No, I thought he wasn't going to kiss me."

A COURTEOUS REBUKE.

"Mine vriendt, I vill gif you seven dollarss—seven larch silver dollarss—for dem diamonds."

"Ah, wot's de matter with youse? I see de reason why youse doesn't eat pork; it's coz you're so much of a hog yerself."

"You go down dot street und ar-r-est yourselluf mit a policeman. I gif you not six dollarss for dose diamonds."

A MEAN REVENGE.

Mrs. Hautry—"You the singing master? But we do not want a singing master."

Herr Pumpernickel—"Barдon; de laty next door told me you wanted one badly. She sent me."

VERY CONSIDERATE.

German professors are proverbially absent-minded, but none of them more so than Prof. Dusel of Bonn. He noticed, one day, his wife placing a large boquet on his desk.

"What does all that mean?" he asked.

"Why, this is the anniversary of your marriage," replied Mrs. Dusel.

"Ach, Gott! Is that so! Well, let me know when yours comes around, and I'll reciprocate."

A German, who was lately married, says, "it vas easier for a needle to valk out of a camel's eye than for a mans to get der lasht vord mit a vomans."

A man's days are numbered, but he cannot recover any of the back numbers.

It is generally the man who can least afford the cost who has the reddest nose.

"I should call the photographer a friend of his race."

"For what reason?"

"He always tries to make people look pleasant who do business with him."

The coalman's season may be the winter, and the summer the iceman's harvest, so that it's possible the milkman finds his greatest profit in the spring.

A sure way to find an old friend is to order a spring chicken at a restaurant.

AND HE WENT NEXT DAY TO THE JEWELER'S.

"Bessie," said the young man, pleadingly, "this is the fourth time I have called at your home since I saw you last. Is there any way by which I can always be sure of finding you in, or at least of always knowing where you are when I call for you?"

"You might ring me up, you know," responded the pretty telephone girl, looking dreamily at her shapely fingers.

A HINT.

Ethel—"George, you remind me of an hour glass."

George—"In what respect?"

Ethel—"The more time given you, the less sand you seem to have."

SO APPROPRIATE.

John Thomas Simkinson knew that he was the accepted lover of Mary Elizabeth Prendergast.

"My own darling!" he exclaimed, rapturously, as he impressed a kiss upon her lips, warmly, yet cautiously, as though he feared rebuke.

She rebuked him not, and he kissed her again. She seemed to like it.

"What shall I call you, love?" he asked.

"Call me?" she replied, queryingly.

"Yes! Don't engaged people have pet names for each other— 'Peaches and Cream', or 'Tootsy-Wootsy,' or some such name?"

"Oh, I see what you mean," the maiden replied; suppose you call me 'Delusion?'"

"'Delusion?'" echoed the young man. "What is the meaning of that? Is it that we are to find our love nothing but a delusion?" he demanded, sternly.

"Not at all."

"Then why do you select that name?"

"Why, John Thomas—because—I understand that men love to—to hug—a delusion."

Then Mr. Simkinson took the happy girl in his arms, and was assured of the correctness of her understanding.

"Yesterday I told Schlegelmayer that his club consisted of block-heads, and to-day I hear that I have been elected an honorary member!"

The boy on the farm approaches his turning period when the haying grindstone is brought out for use.

"I can't sing," said the young lady when invited to warble; but she complied upon being further pressed. When she had finished, Fogg thanked her, and added behind his teeth, "I'll never doubt anybody's word again."

Nothing ever nips the divorce or elopement crops

The desirability of bonds depends on whether you hold them or they hold you.

The college student is apt to find that the beginning comes after the commencement is past.

HIS CHANCE.

Edith—" How cheap I feel ! "
Young Scapely—" Edith, will you be mine ? "

ABOUT THE FRUIT SEASON.

Teacher—" How long did Adam and Eve remain in the Garden of Eden ? "
Boy—" I don't know."
Teacher—" They remained in the Garden of Eden until—until— "
Boy (gleefully)—" Oh, yes ; until the apples were ripe."

THE ENGAGEMENT OVER.

Hilow—" Hello, Glim, how are you ? I haven't seen you in six months."
Glim—" First rate, thank you. How are you ? "
Hilow—Can't complain. How's Miss Dingbats ? You were engaged to her when I left town, I remember." ·
Glim—" We are not engaged now."
Hilow—" Ah, sorry for that, old boy. What was the trouble ? "
Glim—" No trouble. We merely got married."

" She treated me shamefully."
" Ah ! but she treated me worse."
" Impossible ! she jilted me."
" Yes ; but she married me."

City Editor—" Can't you find a new adjective and avoid this constant allusion to people dying at a ' green old age ?' "
Obituary Writer—" I'll try. Suppose I make a distinction and apply the term ' green old-age ' to those between 80 and 90 ; ' ripe old age ' to those between 90 and 100, and mention centenarians as dying at a ' rotten old age.' How'll that do ? "

Clubleigh—" I hear that Dudley is over his head in debt."
Parkleigh—" Is that so ? "
Clubleigh—" Yes, he got that new silk tile of his on credit."

WHAT MADE HER ASK.

"Is there an election campaign going on among the planets, too?" asked Mrs. Snaggs.

"Well, what you are driving at now?" asked her husband in his affectionate manner.

"I saw something in the papers about the opposition of Mars."

CRUSHING.

Ethel (showing her engagement ring)—"Don't you admire his taste?"

Maud—"Y-e-s, so far as jewelry is concerned."

CHRISTIAN UNITY.

Lady parishioner (who is ill and has received many kind attentions from various denominations)—"Father Hightowers, will you please thank Mr. Lowly in my name?"

Father Hightowers (a high-church priest, with his head in the air) —"I—I am sorry to decline, but—I can't do it. He is a Methodist parson."

THE EDITOR'S LOT.

"There are six men down stairs waiting to see the editor."

"Armed?"

"All armed."

"Good! Show'em up. I was afraid they had come to tar and feather me and were going to make me furnish the tar!"

TO BE PUT IN REPAIR.

Footpad (3 a. m.)—"Wot time is it, mister?"

Belated Citizen—Eh—er—my watch dosen't run."

Footpad (producing a revolver)—"Well, you 'ust hand it over ter me an' watch me and it run fur a few seconds."

A TRAGIC TALE OF AN EPISODE BY THE STORM TOSSED MAIN.

They were seated upon the rocky cliffs overlooking a bit of dangerous shore, where a ship had foundered the night before.

The restless waves beat upon the irregular sea wall and sent great flecks of foam high into the air.

Slowly going to pieces upon the cruel rocks, the good ship tossed in in her agony as a delirious patient tosses on his bed of pain.

Ever and anon the green waves dashed over her and drove her firmer into the giant grasp that was crushing the life out of her.

The crew had been safely brought to land and the ship was left to the boisterous caresses of the heartless ocean.

As the young man gazed upon the terrific scene of wind and wave and helpless ship an awestruck silence sealed his lips.

After a few moments thus he turned to the beautiful girl beside him.

A faintly perceptible smile shone in and out amidst the pink and white of her lovely face.

He saw in it the sunshine that lives eternal in the faces of the angels.

She put out her soft, white hand and touched his arm.

He laid his hand tenderly upon hers.

"What is it darling?" he said, in response to her questioning eyes.

"Algernon," she asked, as the breaking waves dashed high, "does the sea wear pants?"

Algernon shuddered and would have fallen, but his will was strong and he stood fast.

"Why do you ask that?" he said, with no answering smile to hers.

"Because, dear," she answered timidly, "because I thought it must, it makes so many breaches over the wreck down there, don't you know.

Then Algernon fell to the earth with a dull thud.

EVEN THERE.

The soul of a former reporter having been ferried over the waters of the Acheron by the boatman Charon, attempted to pass through the gates of Paradise.

"Hold! hold!" cried the good St. Peter. "Where are your credentials?"

"Oh, that is all right," responded the newspaper man, pleasantly, revealing a "Fire-Police" badge; "I am a reporter, you know."

WISDOM'S PROOF.

Billings—"Wilson is a very smart man."

Witherton—"What makes you think so?"

Billings—"He knows as much as his son."

Witherton (with emotion)—"How old is his son!"

Billings—"Just 21."

Witherton (removing his hat)—"What a paragon of wisdom must that parent be."

IN BOSTON.

Boston Child—"Mamma! mamma! The baby has fell out of the window!"

Boston Mother—"'Fallen,' you mean, dear. Quick! run for the doctor!"

A GOOD PLACE.

Robinson—"Where do you do most of your writing, old man?"

Penflinger—"On the railroad, generally."

Robinson—"Why, that's queer! I don't see how you can do it."

Penflinger—"Well, you see, old fellow, my mind's in repose then. No landlord's after me!"

AN UNFORTUNATE PRONUNCIATION.

An energetic German professor was conducting a musical society. They were studying Mendelssohn's "Elijah," and had reached the chorus "Hear us, Baal; hear, mighty God!" The men's voices were booming out sonorously, when the conductor cried out, "No—de dreadful vowel! Don't say B-a-l-e; soften a leetle—give de more musical sound, Bal." Whereupon the chorus took up the strain again, "Hear us, Bawl; hear us, Bawl!"—but they quickly realized the peculiar fitness of the sentiment and broke down in laughter, to the great amazement of the little German, who never saw the joke, but who returned reluctantly to the old pronunciation.

A Dutchman was relating his marvellous escape from drowning when thirteen of his companions were lost by the upsetting of a boat, and he alone was saved. "And how did you escape this fate?" asked one of his hearers. "I tid not co in te pote," was the Dutchman's placid answer.

Fritz is 6. He has a great many brothers and sisters and he prays for them all and for his father and mother and his uncles and aunts and cousins and particular friends every night. He has been in the habit of praying for his mother's visitors, but she has had a lot of company this Summer, and the other night Fritz got tired. He began with "God bless papa" and went bravely through the list till his knees ached. Then he asked: "Mamma, don't you s'pose Mrs. ——'s chillen can take care of 'emselves one night? God an' I have got all we can 'tend to?"

Bertie's father has been very ill and Bertie has not seen him for weeks. Bertie takes off his shoes the minute he comes into the house and puts on the soft slippers he keeps behind the door. But the other night Bertie forgot, he laughed out loud at the foot of the stairs. Bertie's father was a little better, fortunately, and in a few minutes his mother came downstairs. "Papa heard you laugh," she said; "and he wants you to do it again." Every afternoon now Bertie sits on the lowest stair in the hall.

"Say somefin funny, mamma," he begs; "say somefin funny, so I can laugh, and it'll make papa get well to hear me."

Estelle is getting bewildered in the mazes of grammar. Her teacher asked her yesterday to compare the adjective "ill." Estelle did so thus, "ill, worse, dead." Her teacher told of it at the boarding house table and added the story of a boy who conjugated, "go, go it, got there."

Dobbs—"This is rather an expensive umbrella for you to carry. Did you pick it up at a bargain counter?"

Dumper—"Not exactly. I picked it up at a big reception."

Stuart—" I understand that the dropping of Snobberly from the club membership has broken him all up."

Snarleigh—" He must now be in vulgar fractions, then."

John—" I'm going to kiss you, Amy."

Amy (screaming)—" Ow—wo—w."

John—" Great Scott! What was that for? I haven't kissed you yet."

Amy—" But I thought I'd have that part of it over and done with."

Madison (meeting Johnson on the pier)—" What, you here, after telling me you didn't expect to enjoy a vacation this Summer?"

Johnson—" But I'm not enjoying it; my wife's along."

Country Cousin—" Why don't you try bathing your face in milk?"

City Cousin—" Oh, because chalk always makes my face dreadfully rough."

" I hear that in the slugging match McCabe was worsted."

" Oh, that's a yarn."

AN AWFUL EXAMPLE OF HIMSELF.

Street fakir—" 'Ere y'are, dow: 'Ostetter's Patedt Balsab! Cures ady case of coughs (atchoo!) ad colds."

Observant idler—" What are you giving us? You've got such a cold yourself you can hardly croak."

Street fakir—" That's all right. I got it od purpose so I could cure it to-borrow id presedce of the public. 'Ere y'are, dow. Fifty cedts a bottle! "

A MARRIAGE INDICATION.

Worried Wife—" Darling, why do you not pay me the little attentions you used to before we were married?"

Happy Husband—" Did you ever see anyone run after a horse car when he had caught it?"

CAUSE FOR SORROW.

Levi—" Vot makes you look so sorrowful, Chake?'

Cohen—" I chust now soldt a two tollar coat to a Irishman for six tollars, and he didn't dry to knocgk me down; I'm kicgkin' myself begause I didn't asgk ten."

INQUISITIVE JIMMY.

Little Jimmy—" Let me see your shoes, won't you, Mr. Doingwell?"

Mr. Doingwell—" Why, what do you want to see my shoes for?"

Little Jimmy—" 'Course I heard pop tellin' sis the other day that you was "well heeled," and I want to see what kind they are."

What is the difference between a young woman who refuses a flower when offered by a lover, and a man out on a cold night without adequate protection?

One snubs his rose and the other rubs his nose.

Carleton—"Gad, what a pretty girl!"

Montauk—"Girl's not much; the cob, though, is certainly 'hansom.'"

Buyer—"Is this suit all wool?"

Mozinsky—"I von't lie to you, my frient, it is not; de buttons vas made of silgk."

Miss Hytes—"I don't see what you see in that Will Chumpley."

Miss Hylle—"I am preparing an essay on 'Quintescent Inanity' and am using him as a model."

Augustus—"Is Ballantyne a good mimic?"

Montague—"First class; I saw him imitate the mixing of a cocktail once and it put such an edge on my appetite that I ate a boarding house steak with a relish."

He (clasping her to his manly bosom)—"Do you love me, darling?"

She—"Well, I have a leaning toward you, Gerold."

Lucie—"Ned made a ringing speech last night, mamma."

Mamma—"Um——um?"

Lucie—"He asked me to be his wife."

Officer Zcermlomski (who has come to the Bilkins' residence from the scene of a painful accident)—"Is this Mrs. Bilkins, mum?"

Mrs. Bilkins—"Yes."

Officer Zcermlomski—"Well, I've been sent to tell you that your husband's head has been bruk in, mum, and I'm to break it to you gently, mum."

Chappie—"What's the mattah, dear boy?"

Cholly—"Nothing much—bwain fever."

Chappie—"Good heaven—that's fatal!"

Cholly—"Usually, dear boy, but (superiorly) the docter said there was no danger with such a physique as I have."

Deacon Jones—"Why, man alive, you are wrong, entirely wrong. You know what the Bible says?"

Bass—"No, I can't say that I do. I knew the book was out, but haven't had time to read it yet."

Masculine voice (from the dim, dark corner)—"Why do you put cold cream on your lips?" And the funny part was that the man couldn't see an inch before his face.

"You are charged with running along the sidewalk at a rapid rate and knocking people down," said the police justice.

"Well, I have right to, haven't I?" saucily answered the prisoner.

"No, sir; you have not. If you want to do that sort of thing you must own a bicycle."

Watts—"I usually manage to swallow most of these newspaper stories, but when they tell of an Indian in New Mexico digging his way out of jail with two toothpicks, I weaken.

Potts—"I guess you never saw a New Mexico toothpick."

HIS REASON.

She is charming and stylish and clever,
    She is fair as a flower, and young
As a morning in May. No one ever
    To a lovelier creature hath sung.

Her beauty possesses a glory
    That makes my heart quiver and throb.
But I never will tell her my story,
    For I've seen her eat corn off the cob.

A HIT AT THE CLOTH.

Minister (to tailor)—"You have cut the vest wrong, Mr. Misfit. I wanted it to button close about the neck. This is the style that any gentleman wears."

Mr. Misfit—"Yes; it's my mistake. You wanted a minister's vest, and I've gone and cut a gentleman's vest. But I guess I can fix it."

ANTICIPATING HIM.

Mr. Lurker—"Excuse me, Miss Snapper, but I have long sought this opportunity to—"

Miss Snapper—"Never mind the preamble Mr. Lurker. Run right along in and ask pa. He's been expecting this would come for the last two years."

A CHEERFUL ASSOCIATION.

"Upon my word!" exclaimed young Dr. Caraway, raising his glasses and looking intently at one of the boxes. "She's a perfect image, line for line, of the girl."

"What girl are you talking about?" asked Hooks.

"The one we had a clinic on this morning," the doctor said, without removing the glasses.

Dancing master—"I want to look at some nice shoes for dancing."

Shoe man—"Yes, sir, here you are, a nice pair of kangaroo skin shoes—and you know, sir, for hops the kangaroo can't be beaten."

"When it comes to making a lining for a nest," softly quacked the eider duck, "I've got it down fine."

The Editor — "I like this poem; it is capital."
The Poet — "Yes, I hope so; but—how much?"

Clubson — "Is Spongely much given to drink?"
Treatly — "Quite the reverse."
Clubson — "What? a total abstainer?"
Treatly — "No; much drink is given to Spongely."

Reporter — "I hear there has been another railroad accident?"
Superintendent — "No; only a railroad incident—two trains collided."

> On Greenland's icy mountains,
> That's where I want to be,
> In weather, when the mercury
> Abides at ninety-three.
> For some sweet maiden Eskimo,
> I'd swap Bess, Nell or Cora,
> And at her daddy's igloo gate
> We'd study the aurora.

"I saw you at the play last night."
"Yes, it was Mary Ann's night in."

Some men are born wealthy; some men are born great;
But all men are kicking forever at Fate.

An incorrigible office-seeker died a few years ago and his friends asked a well-known journalist for an epitaph for his tombstone.
The journalist suggested the following, which was not, however, adopted:

HERE LIES JOHN JONES
IN THE ONLY PLACE FOR WHICH HE
NEVER APPLIED.

The policeman can get along better with a tough if he knows how to take him.

Of all the methods or capital punishment the guillotine still takes the head.

A man is called a confirmed liar when nothing that he says is confirmed.

The lambs gambol on the green, and it's only a question of time when they get fleeced.

The cold water organization won't fuse with any party, but they mightn't object to forming a pool.

"See here, waiter, this pie hasn't any apples in it!"
Waiter—"I know it, sah; it am made of evaporated apples."

> There was a printer who loved a maid,
> He put her form to press;
> And, as 'twas badly justified,
> 'Twas pied to her distress.

"Is it true, Miss Gertie," he said, "there are just two things a woman will jump at—a conclusion and a mouse?"
"No," she answered. "There is a third."
After thinking the matter over a few moments he tremblingly made her an offer, but she didn't jump at it. He was not the right man.

Mamma—"Don't you know that your father is the mainstay of the family?"
Freddy—"Golly, ain't he though; and the spanker too."

Junkman—"Rags! Rags! Rags!"
Tatterdon Torne (just passing)—"Don't yer git so all fired personal in yer remarks."

"This climate of yourn hain't no great shakes ez I can see."
Arkansas Native—"You wait till our ager gits you, and I guess you'll change yer mind, stranger.

TO BE SEEN.

"Put on some more clothes, Mandy!" shrieked the elderly aunt at the watering place; "folks will see you," she added, horror struck.
"Aunt Julia," replied Amanda as she went out among the waves with all the trustful innocence of a Texas statesman, "what are we here for?"

A DECEITFUL GIRL.

Miss Russell—"I think Jennie Oldham is just as mean as she can be."
Miss Brown—"Why, what's she done?"
Miss Russell—"She's given it out that her uncle's taken her to Bar Harbor and Newport for the summer, yet she's only sitting out in the back yard every hot day to get her face tanned."

SLIGHT MISUNDERSTANDING.

A Texas Sheriff, with papers in a civil suit, entered the house of an attractive widow and said:

"Madam, I have an attachment for you."

The widow blushed, but said something about reciprocation.

"You must proceed to court."

"I prefer that you do that "——

"Come, hurry, please, the Justice is waiting."

"Oh, well, then you have the license, I suppose?"

The Sheriff cleared himself in time.

A REAL ARTIST.

Claribel—"So you are engaged, I hear, Mabel? Who is the man?"

Mabel—"Oh, he's a charming fellow; an artist."

Claribel—"What, one of those poor men who draw?"

Mabel—"He draws, but he isn't so awfully poor."

Claribel—"He must be, Mabel. They all are. What kind of drawing does he do?"

Mabel—"The very nicest kind, Claribel. He draws checks, and the bank pays him cash for them right on the spot."

Claribel—Er—er—um. Let me compliment you, Mabel, on your artistic taste."

———

She—"It's leap year—will you marry me?"

He (nervously)—"I—O—"

She (calmly)—"How much?"

———

If a boy is well thrashed he ought to be "as good as wheat."

———

Did any one ever see a woman who could look intelligent while talking to a baby?

———

It's only in the order of events that when his best girl shakes a fellow he's rattled.

———

"A hare in the garden! Hand me a gun, Jacques."

"But, sir, it is 5 in the morning; everybody is asleep."

"Never mind; I'll fire on tiptoe."

———

"It was scandalous the way Dobbs flirted with his wife."

"Why shouldn't a man flirt with his wife?"

"Ah—but she was his first wife, and they were divorced."

———

"Your wife is a very decided blonde, isn't she?"

"Decided! You would be quite sure of it if you came to our house often."

She—"It certainly must mean something when a man puts a diamond ring on a girl's finger."

He (of hard experience)—"It means that he owes some jeweler two or three hundred dollars."

Young Housekeeper—"Please send up a pound of calf's liver."

Butcher—"Very sorry, miss, but we have no veal to-day."

Young Housekeeper (liftily)—"I didn't ask for veal; I said (distinctly) calf's liver."

"What's this," asked Mrs. Gimp, as she looked at a dwarf on exhibition at the museum.

"That's a minute man," replied her husband.

"Have you any Madrigals?" asked a musician as he stepped into a Detroit music store.

"Madri-gals?" echoed the new clerk, "what do you take us for? We don't keep an intelligence office," and he smiled superciliously on the astonished customer.

An engagement ring on the finger does not make it certain that a wedding is on hand.

Fangle—"Oh, there are no masters of the art of writing fiction nowadays."

Cumso—"You are not reading this year's circus posters evidently."

"Well," said the Chicago citizen who looked at a drop of water through a microscope, "that is what I call pretty rough on a man who has sworn off."

She (to Cousin George, who has just returned from the tropics)—"O George, dear, how kind of you to bring me this dear little monkey! How thoughtful you are! But—but it is just like you!"

The next thing after a sweet girl graduating essay is usually a very successful essay on man.

A frog is always in the spring of life.

After the pickpocket has succeeded in getting his hand in he takes things easily.

People who imagine the average messenger boy can do nothing quick will be surprised to learn that one has been discovered fast asleep.

"There!" she said, standing on her tiptoes, "I am about your size."
"On the contrary," said the disconsolate lover, "my sighs are about you."

A poor old toper, who was in the habit of getting lost on his way home, was asked how he could afford to keep the dog that was always with him. "That dog," he said, "not only boards himself but finds me."

Paul, aged five, carries water for the chickens. At breakfast one day an egg was too soft for him. After looking at it a moment he cried out: "Mamma, these chickens have been having too much water."

Tom—"Miss Trills has a voice of great compass."
Dick—"Is that what's the matter? I wish she'd box it."

A thing of beauty is a joy until it goes in bathing.

"Do you pretend to have as good a judgment as I have?" exclaimed an enraged wife to her husband.
"Well, no," he replied slowly, "our choice of partners for life shows that my judgment is not to be compared with yours."

"Is this a picture of you?"
"Yes. That's me."
"That's bad grammar."
"I know it. It's a bad picture, too."

A lady was asked, "At what age were you married?" She was equal to the emergency and quietly responded, "At the parsonage."

Borus—"Young Ardup doesn't seem to have any bad habits. That at least redounds to his everlasting credit."
Mr. Howell (of the firm of Gettup & Howell)—"Not at this store. Thirty days is the limit with us."

Bixley—"Is that very stout lady Billings' wife?"
Hixley—"Yes."
Bixley—"Every now and then you find a man who draws a large figure in the lottery of marriage."

SENTIMENT SPOILED.

In the promenade.
"We keep step perfectly," murmered Wadsleigh.

"Yes," with a sigh.

"Well, darling—may I call you so? I want to ask you to walk with me through life."

"Thank you, but I've already accepted an invitation to ride."

ALL RIGHT IN THIS CASE.

It was 11:50 Saturday night, and the lovely young heiress of $5,000,000 said to her adorer:

"Harold, papa looks with favor upon you, but—but I think it best to tell you that—that he is a firm advocate of Sunday closing."

And Harold reached for his hat.

POLITE, THOUGH A BRIDE.

At a wedding recently, when the officiating clergyman put to the lady the question: " Wilt thou have this man to be thy wedded husband?" she dropped the prettiest courtesy, and, with a modesty which lent her beauty an additional grace, replied: "If you please."

SHE DIDN'T TAKE.

"What do you take me for, anyhow?" queried Chappie, when Ethel asked him to swim out in the surf and get her parasol, which had blown away.

"I don't take you for anything," said she, "and wouldn't if you proposed a million times."

NO CINCH FOR THE LANDLORD.

"George," as they sat in the sands, "isn't it a solemn thing to reflect how for thousands of years this great sea has washed the beach, and how it will continue for thousands of years after we are gone?"

"Yes; but a pleasanter thought occurs to me."

"What is it, dear?"

"The landlord of this hotel hasn't such a cinch on his surroundings."

How to get inside information: Use a stomach pump.

For a full crop on the farm commend us to the old hen.

The stooping bicycle rider may be supposed to be on pleasure bent.

Father—"What are you practising with my daughter now?"
Music Master—"Patience."

Unconscious Wisdom: "Is your father a musician?"
"No, indeed; he writes operas."

A bee that buzzed a young lady by the seashore got an instant mash.

As another proof of woman's inability to keep a secret we notice that while a man covers his suspenders a woman wears hers openly.

As quoted by young Lovers: So-fa and no father.

Tommy—" Uncle Jack, I often hear them talking about safe burglars; what do they mean by that kind of burglar?"

Uncle Jack—" There is only one kind of a safe burglar, my boy. He's the one that's in jail."

Effie—" There are as fine fish in the sea as ever were caught."

Blanche—" Yes; but they don't do anything but watch the little ones nibble."

" Why do you irritate mamma so, George?"

" Because, my dear, I hope some day to make her speechless with indignation."

She—" Then you'll take me for a drive on Thursday?"

He—" Yes, but suppose it rains."

She—" Come the day before, then."

WHAT THE DOCTOR WAS GOOD FOR.

" Doctor, I want to thank you for your great patent medicine."

" It helped you, did it?" asked the doctor very much pleased.

" It helped me wonderfully."

" How many bottles did you find it necessary to take?"

" Oh, I didn't take any of it. My uncle took one bottle, and I am his sole heir."

SHE WAS CONSIDERATE.

As an old woman was lately walking through one of the streets in the country at midnight, a patrol called out:

" Who's there?"

" It is I, patrol," she replied, " don't be afraid."

A HOLMES EPIGRAM ON TEAS.

This story is told by Oliver Wendell Holmes:

When her lion was leaving the hostess, who had put the cream of her acquaintance on parade and rather expected effusive admiration from the great man, said, with a confidential smile: " Well, Dr. Holmes, what do you think of afternoon tea?"

He answered in these four striking, graphic words: " It is giggle—gabble—gobble and git!"

THE DEAR GIRLS.

She—"Would you believe that I have no fewer than five young men on my hands at the present time?"

Blanche (glancing at Sue's hands)—"Yes, dear, I can readily believe it."

Young lady (in candy store)—"I don't like this candy. It has begun to melt already."

Confectioner—"No wonder, young lady, with those liquid eyes of yours over it!"

"Six pounds please."

"I see they have started another lodge of the Improved Order of the Red Men in your village."

"Yes, my husband has joined it. But that is not the kind of order needed in our midst."

"No?"

"No; what is wanted is an improved order of white men."

A very seedy individual, with his trousers worn thin behind and before, appeared one day in the office of the late Gen. C. B. Fiske and laid claim to his charity on the ground that they were both Methodists. "Oh, yes," said the General, after looking at him for a moment, "I see you are a Methodist. You have the marks. You wore out your trousers at the knees praying and you wore them out behind backsliding."

"I recently performed four marriage ceremonies in twenty minutes," remarked the Rev. Mr. Thirdly.

"That was at the rate of twelve knots an hour," added Miss Flyp.

First Pullman Porter—"Whad's yo' ser nervous 'bout, Johns'n?"

Second Porter—"I'se a quartah out. Dat's what I'se nervous 'bout. Done blacked a pah ob my own boots by mistake fer dat nabob's in d' fo'th suction."

BOTH SIDES OF THE CASE.

She—"I was calling on Miss Dingle the other night, and she said she thought you were an awfully pretty girl."

She—"That's strange. Mr. Wayback told me she said I was positively plain."

She—"She evidently didn't know that you knew him."

HE LOVED PIE.

A woman had a pair of twin sons so closely alike in looks and voice that often, when she was not paying particular attention, she herself was liable to mistake one for the other.

One day, after the twins had been playing several hours out of doors together, one of them—whose name might have been Jacob—came into the house and said:

"Mother, I'm hungry; I want a piece of pie."

Without noticing which it was, she gave him the pie, which he immediately took around the corner of the house and ate; then returning, he said in an aggrieved tone:

"Mother, I want a piece of pie."

All went well until poor Esau came in a few minutes afterward, only to discover how both he and his mother had been cheated.

THE WAY OUT.

Angelina Hamfatte—"It's no use. We can't draw, I've got a divorce, I've scratched my rival, I've lost my diamonds and found them. Now what can I do to make the miserable people come?"

Her Manager—"Act a little."

HIS START WAS WRONG.

Mr. Potts—"A great strapping lout like you begging for food! You ought to be ashamed of yourself."

Weary Watkins—"I am, pardner, I am. If I'd a-had any git-up about me at all I'd 'a' been borned rich."

WAITING.

My name is Ebenezer—
'Tis a name I much despise;
And, oh, how quick I'll drop it
When rich Uncle Ebbie dies!

An old negro preacher divided his sermon into two parts: "First, all de things in de text; and second, all de things not in de text; and, bredren, we'll wrastle wid de second part fust."

A temperance lecturer, descanting on the superior virtues of cold water, remarked: "When the world had become so corrupt that the Lord could do nothing with it, He was obliged to give it a thorough sousing in cold water."

"Yes," replied a toper present, "but it killed every critter on the face of the earth."

Norman MacLeod was once preaching in a district in Ayrshire, where the reading of a sermon was regarded as the greatest fault of which the minister could be guilty. When the congregation dispersed, an old woman, overflowing with enthusiasm, addressed her neighbor: "Did ye ever hear onything sae gran'? Wasna that a sermon?"

"Oh, ay," replied her friend, sulkily, "but he read it."

"Read it!" said the other, with indignant emphasis, "I wadna hae cared if he had whustled it."

Dorothy (aged 3) to her older sister—"I'm as tall as you."

Marjorie—"No, you're not. Stand up and see. There, you only come to my mouth."

Dorothy—"Well, I don't care. I'm as tall the other way; my feet go down as far as yours."

"Goodness gracious, child! That book isn't fit for you to read!"

"It is just the thing for this weather, mamma. It is so delightfully wicked that it keeps the cold chills running over me all the time."

"It is the little things that worry a man," remarked the father of a family of girls, as he paid a large bill for his daughters' bathing suits.

The world may owe us a living, but it hasn't authorized anybody to settle debts of that kind.

Maud—"I do wish that good clothes were just like bad habits."

Stella—"Oh, why, dear?"

Maud—"Because then they would grow on us and save so much expense and worry."

She—"I'm going to the beach, and want to get some sort of a bathing costume. Most of these are ludicrous, you know. Can't you suggest something that will prevent me from making a fright of myself?"

He—"You might keep beneath the surface of the water."

Plenty will have to give up her horn before the prohibitionists will admit that she is truly good.

Mr. Huckleberry—"No one admires me."

Miss Wallflower—"No one admires me, either."

Mr. Huckleberry—"We had better organize a mutual admiration society. I admire your eyes. What do you admire about me?"

Miss Wallflower—"Your good taste."

Mamma—"Arthur, didn't I tell you to take those powders every two hours?"

Little Arthur—"Yes; but you never told me where you wanted me to take them to."

McDab—"What we want is a pleasant Summer home where we can escape the heat. Are the nights chilly?"

Landlord—"Heavens! yes! we have ague here the year round."

Mollie—"Whatever induced you to take this horrid-looking material for a dress?"

Ethel—"It is the only way I can be sure of getting back what is left over at the dressmaker's."

Bell Boy—"The man in 24 has committed suicide."
Clerk—"Did he blow out the gas?"
Bell Boy—"No, he had blown in his money."

"How did Slopace come to kill himself?"
Pollock—"The doctor told him he had quick consumption, and he was afraid he might have to hurry."

Parton—"Did your son study medicine as you planned for him to?"
Father—"Oh, no; he is a specialist."

Daisy—"I wonder how it is that Mrs. Totterby is such a good traveler, when she looks so frail?"
Dashaway—"There is nothing strange in it; her husband gets passes."

Poet (disconsolately receiving the inevitable "unavailable")—"This is tough!"
Editor (blandly)—"Just so; it's stuff!"

Julia—"Are you real well acquainted with Mr. Bricktop?"
Hattie—"No, not exactly. You see we were only engaged for one week last Summer."

Watts—"If I had only thought of it earlier in the season, I might have had a million of 'em on the market by now."
Potts—"A million of what?"
Watts—"Flannel shirts lined with wire gauze. They couldn't shrink, don't you see?"

"Cruickshanks is passionately fond of bicycle riding."
"Yes. I fancied as I saw him take a 'header' last evening, that he must be heels over head in love with it."

Shingiss (seeing his friend Van Braam emerge from a barber's shop)—"Did you have a dry shampoo?"
Van Braam—"No; I expected the barber would talk himself dry, but he didn't."

Rowne DeBout—"I saw a remarkable sign in a window when I was in France."
Stayatt Holmes—"What was it?"
Rowne DeBout—"American French spoken here."

"I want my rights," fiercely shouted the bass-voiced woman from the platform at the woman suffrage meeting.

"You can have 'em," piped her husband's timid voice from a far-away corner. "Here's the twins, and I'll go to the neighbors and gather up the other six."

AN ULTIMATUM.

They sat together in the kitchen, the servant girl and the blue-coated policeman.

Her cheek was close to his brass-buttoned breast, and his hand toyed nervously with the knot in her apron strings.

They talked in low, earnest tones, and shot glances full of undying love into each other's eyes. Such communions of soul are sacred, and their more private conversation will not be revealed here. At length the sighing swain glanced at the clock, and, rising slowly, and regretfully, remarked:

"I must go pull the box."

"But what shall I do?" wailed the poor girl, clinging to his arm.

"Ah, that's easy, see? You just tell the old lady that if she fires ye, I'll arrest 'er husban' the next time 'e comes 'ome wit a jag."

WISHED TO ADJOURN.

Penelope—"Pa, please don't kill Reginald. He loves me."

Reginald—"Dear, good sir, don't kick me out. I was not aware it was so late. Give me a chance and I'll go."

Old Man—"Hold. I ask thee not to go. I've waited three hours to give thee my blessing and merely dropped in to say that I cannot keep myself awake longer. I ask for adjournment to another date."

WHAT SHE WANTED WITH IT.

Wife—"I want a new dress, George."

Husband (curtly)—"And what do you want with a new dress, I'd like to know?"

Wife (pleasantly)—"I want to wear it, George. Did you think I wanted it to wave in the atmosphere to scare the hawks away from the chickens?"

DISTINCTION WITHOUT DIFFERENCE.

He—"I don't like Mrs. Snapper."

She—"Why not?"

He—"Because she is too blunt."

She—"Too blunt? Why, I thought she was extremely sharp."

HE WASN'T EXALTED.

They were rehearsing for the wedding. The organ had ceased it's roaring, and the bride and groom stood with clasped hands before the altar. There was a holy stillness throughout the sacred edifice and the solemnity of the sanctuary exalted almost all the hearts of the group gathered at the chancel.

The most notable exception was the heart of the professional master of ceremonies.

It was not exalted to any appreciable extent.

" Do you take this woman to be " —

The master of ceremonies critically contemplated the happy pair.

"— your wedded — don't squeeze hands — wife ? "

The groom's lips moved.

" Don't open your mouth too wide."

The groom looked scared and whispered something.

" Look pleasant, please — do you take this man to be your wedded — the chin a little higher — husband — eyes not quite so much obscured — there."

The bride trembled and gasped unintelligibly.

"Will you cherish, protect — a little more on the right foot — and defend — look to the altar — until death doth — not quite so much bend in the knee — part ? "

The groom nervously signified that he would.

" Will you love — don't be thinking how your dress hangs — honor and — don't get too close to the groom — obey ? "

"Yes," ventured the bride.

" Don't make the responses too confidently — whom God hath joined let no man — don't exchange glances — put asunder."

The organ roared again. The party wended its way from the church, but the exaltion was in a measure abated.

SMART BOY.

Little Dick — "There goes Johnny Smart on a safety. He's the brightest boy in town."

Father — " How so ? "

Little Dick — " He got himself a rich father.'

Father — " Humph! I don't understand."

Little Dick — " Why his real father died, an' then an' orful rich man got acquainted with his mother, but he didn't like Johnny; so Johnny pretended he was sick and goin' to die; then after the rich man married his mother he got well."

In Ireland, recently, a quarrel had taken place at a fair, and a culprit was being sentenced for manslaughter. The doctor, however, had given evidence to show that the victim's skull was abnormally thin. The prisoner, on being asked if he had anything to say for himself, replied: "No, Yer Honor; but I would ask was that a skull for a man to go to a fair with ? "

Excited Lady (on the beach) — " Why isn't something done for that ship in distress? Why don't some of you —— "

Coast Guard (hurriedly) — " We have sent the crew a line to come ashore, mum."

Excited Lady — " Good gracious! Were they waiting for a formal invitation ? "

One-fingered Jake
Thus spake :
"Bill—he wuz raw—
He said 'twas a buz saw.
I said he lied,
'N then I tried
T' p'int out to him
Along its rim
Thar wan't no teeth in sight—
    Zipp!
    Flip!
Bill was right."

" I wish to get a boy's suit ; the strongest you have."

"Here, madam, are some goods that will stand anything except tobogganing on a barbed wire fence."

" Um—a boy couldn't go tobogganing on a barbed wire fence, could he?"

"No, madam."

"Then perhaps they'll do."

A notice of a recent steamboat explosion in a Western paper ends as follows : "The captain swam ashore. So did the chambermaid. She was insured for $15,000 and loaded with iron."

Mr. Blingo—"You want to be careful about packing away your Winter clothes, my dear. The moths are likely to get into them."

Mrs. Blingo—"You needn't be alarmed about the moths. They are not going to bother with plush when they can get genuine seal-skin at the woman's who lives next door."

Cora—"Why are you going to marry that big ugly captain?"

Dora—"It is against the law, you know, to resist an officer."

"Do you like the dinner, John?" anxiously inquired his wife. "I cooked it all myself."

"Ye-es," said John, trying to be kind and truthful at once, "but I am afraid, dear, that there must be some misprints in the cook book you use."

Doting Father (to college president)—"Give my son a careful training in foot ball. I want him to be a superb kicker. I am a mugwump myself."

Customer—"I want a clock to run thirty days."

Jeweler (politely)—"I'm sorry to disappoint you, sir; but we conduct an exclusively cash business."

Yabsley—" Made any election bets yet, Mudge ? "
Mudge—" Only a hat."
Yabsley—" Which size, morning or evening ? "

The Microbe Crank—" Aren't you going to kiss me ? " she asked, as they parted at the gate.
" I—I cannot, dear," he sadly sighed. " You have not been boiled."

AN ESSAY ON MAN.

Behold the drinker, by some peculiar law,
Pleased with a bottle, tickled with a straw.

A DELAYED CHRISTENING.

Rubenstein—" Vat you gif der baby dis year ? "
Feldkahn—"Ach, ve vos shly like foxes. Ve vait till Grismas unt gif him his name."

AN EVEN CHANCE.

Bank President—" You will have to go to Canada alone ; I shall give myself up."
Cashier—" If you do, you will go to State prison."
Bank President—" Well, it's a toss-up; and I've been to Canada."

HE STILL WAITS.

To him who waits all things will come, no matter what his wish may
Be.
But the waiter deft is waiting yet who waiteth for a tip from
Me.

" Whatever made you make Brackins a present of a pocket comb? He's as bald as a billiard ball."
" That's just it; I want to make him think I never noticed it."

Wings—" Poor Fulites is dead, but in his time he was a leading actor in many moving scenes."
Flies—" Yes; he was the best scene shifter I ever met."

Dudsleigh—" Do you like cycling with a party ? "
Wheelsbee—" No; I prefer to cyclone."

Mrs. Quimper (who has never been at sea before)—" It's very queer, Rufus, but I have a sort of sinking feeling. Do you ? "
Mr. Quimper (laconically)—" No; mine's a risin' one."

SHE WAS FORGIVEN.

Young Husband—"Why, my dear; this pudding is burnt black. How did that happen?"

Young Wife—"I'm sure I don't know. I looked at it just before you came home and it was all right."

"But I've been home two hours."

"Dear me! I thought it was only a few minutes.'

THE FOREIGN VOTE.

Citizen—"These ignorant foreigners should not be allowed to vote."

Statesman—"That's just what I was thinkin'. Half of 'em look so much alike I can't tell which ones I've given two dollar bills to, an' which ones I haven't."

THE MUGWUMP GOAT.

First Goat—"You look angry, William."

Second Goat—"I am. I ordered a lot of imported cans for dinner last night and they sent me American tin plate, instead."

BADLY TANGLED.

"Chi–chi–children," began the timid young man who had just been appointed Superintendent of the Sabbath School. "Of course you are all familiar with the story of the swallow that whaled Jonah — er — er — I mean the swale that wallowed Jonah — er — er — that is, the whale that Jonahed — um — um — um — the Jollow that wonahed the swale — I mean — er — the Jail that swallowed wonah — er — er — gug — gug —" (*Chokes.*)

"I presume, Brother Sims," said the Collection-taker, kindly, "you mean the Jonah that swallowed the — er — er — that is —"

"Ye-Yes, sir," responded the timid young man; "that is what I mean."

AN EARLY BEGINNING.

Mrs. Ananias—"What kind of a man do you expect to make, if you continue to tell stories?"

Willy Ananias—"Oh, a second Chauncey M. Depew, perhaps!"

SHE WAS USED TO HUGGING.

"But weren't you dreadfully scared, Miss Flypp, when the bear got his arm around you?" asked Mr. Maddox.

"Oh, dear, no," replied Miss Flypp. "I was once engaged to a Pittsburg young man."

A BITTER DISAPPOINTMENT.

Mrs. Redrivers—"And that, Mrs. Clum, is the whole story of the affair from beginning to end."

WEHMAN BROS.'

—BOOK OF—

125 CARD TRICKS

PRICE 30 CENTS.

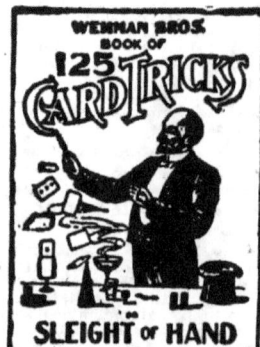

ADDRESS ALL ORDERS DIRECT TO
WEHMAN BROS., 158 Park Row, New York.

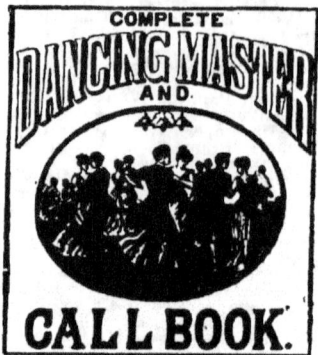